MONSTER MATHS

MONEY

WRITTEN BY

MADELINE TYLER

ILLUSTRATED BY

AMY LI

BookLife
PUBLISHING

©2020
BookLife Publishing Ltd.
King's Lynn
Norfolk PE30 4LS

ISBN: 978-1-83927-108-3

Written by:
Madeline Tyler

Edited by:
John Wood

Designed/Illustrated by:
Amy Li

All rights reserved.
Printed in Malaysia.

PHOTO CREDITS

All images courtesy of Shutterstock. With thanks to Getty Images, Thinkstock Photo and iStockphoto.

Cover, Page 1 & Page 2 – memphisslim, jojje, Dmitrijj Skorobogatov, Abscent, ag1100. Master Images – jojje (grid), Dmitrijj Skorobogatov (illustration texture), Abscent (pattern), ag1100 (paper texture), wk1003mike (wood texture), arigato (carpet texture), cluckva (wallpaper texture), janniwet, letovsegda (coin shine), Amy Li (all illustrations). P3 – Jacob_09, Kriengsuk Prasroetsung, Sko Olena¬, p4–5 – fotomirk, Corey Frey, Valeriya_Do, p6–7 – Loveinthat, p10–11,15,21,24 (Sweet Bag) – Africa Studio, Ksenia_designer, Madlen, nelea33, timquo, p10, 12_13, 15_16, 19, 21 (Shop) – Teerapun, RODINA OLENA, p10, 16–18, 21, 24 (Cuddly monster) – Corey Frey, p16–17 – Valeriya_Do, p22–23 – Loveinthat, Larienn, iliveinoctober, PrasongTakham, p24 – Larienn, iliveinoctober , Valeriya_Do, Svjatoslav Andreichyn

COVENTRY LIBRARIES

Please return this book on or before
the last date stamped below.

To renew this book take it to any of
the City Libraries before
the date due for return

Coventry City Council

Tickles wants to buy her brother, Pod, a present.

Pod likes monster sweets
and monster treats...

4

... and cuddly monsters with spiky horns!

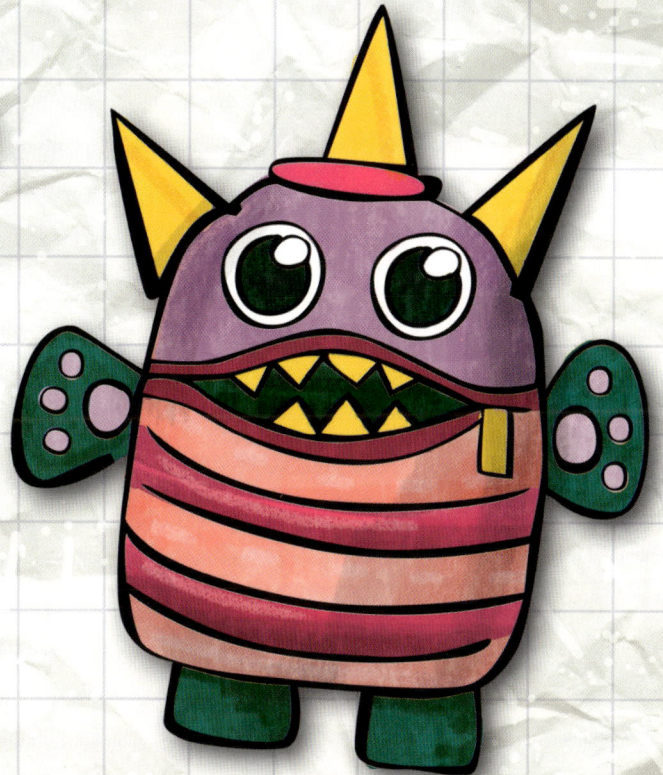

Tickles has lots of coins.

Tickles has 5 growls and 8 rumbles.

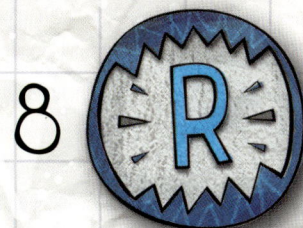

1 G 2 G

3 G 4 G 5 G

1 R 2 R 3 R 4 R

5 R 6 R 7 R 8 R

7

These coins are round.

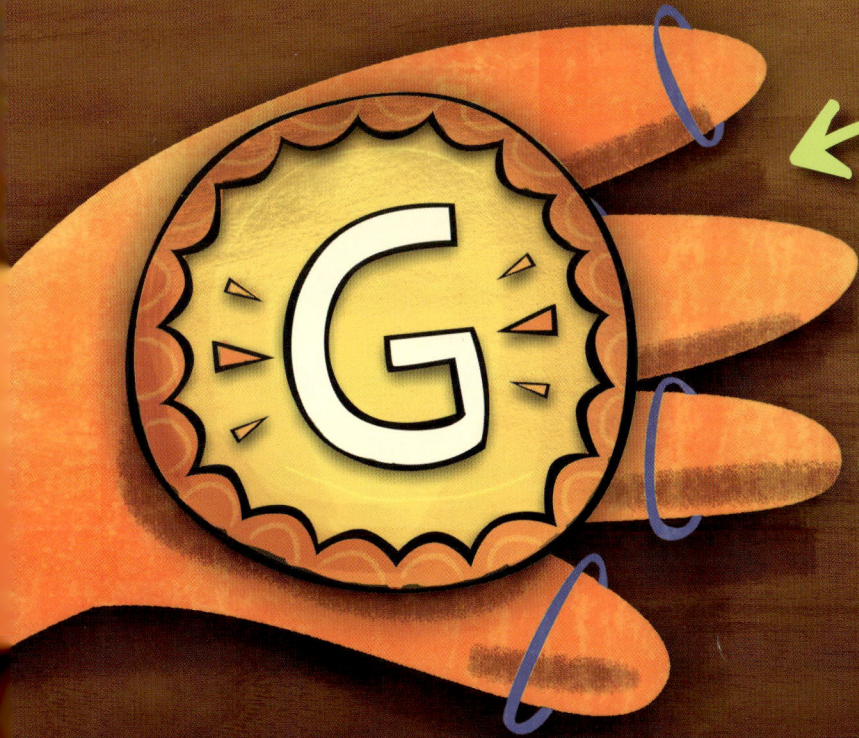

Some coins are big.

Some coins are small.

What shall she buy?

GUM = 1 RUMBLE

MONSTER MART

Monster sweets cost 2 growls and 3 rumbles.

How many growls does Tickles need?

G G

$$1 + 1 = 2$$

How many rumbles does Tickles need?

$$1 + 1 + 1 = 3$$

Does Tickles have enough coins?

Yes, she does!

GUM = 1 RUMBLE

RT

But look – a cuddly monster!

Pod loves cuddly monsters!

This cuddly monster costs 3 growls and 5 rumbles.

Can you count the growls and rumbles?

$$1 + 1 + 1 = 3$$

$$1 + 1 + 1 + 1 + 1 = 5$$

Does Tickles have enough coins?

Yes, she does!

GUM = 1 RUMBLE

21

Tickles has spent all her money.

She bought monster sweets and a cuddly monster.

TO: POD

TO: POD

23

Pod loves his presents!
Well done, Tickles.